Green Revolution: Cultivating the Future without Soil

Comprehensive Guide to Hydroponics and Aquaponics: Techniques, Innovations, and Strategies for Sustainable and Profitable Agriculture.

Geremy Green

1. Introduction to Hydroponics and Aquaponics

   • Definition and key differences.

   • Brief history and development of the techniques.

2. Basic Principles of Hydroponics

   • How hydroponics works.

   • Advantages and challenges of hydroponics.

3. Basic Principles of Aquaponics

   • Integration of fish and plants.

   • Benefits of the symbiotic ecosystem.

4. Essential Components and Equipment
   • Reservoir, pumps, lights, substrates.
   • Monitoring tools and maintenance.

5. Popular Hydroponic Systems

- DWC (Deep Water Culture), NFT (Nutrient Film Technique), and others.

  - Pros and cons of each system.

6. Setting Up an Aquaponic System

  - Choosing fish and plants.

  - Balancing the ecosystem.

7. Nutrition and pH: Crucial Growth Factors

  - Balancing nutrients in both systems.
  - The importance of pH monitoring.

8. Pest and Disease Management

  - Prevention and treatment in a soilless environment.

  - Organic and sustainable approaches.

9. Integrating Hydroponics and Aquaponics

- Creating hybrid systems for maximizing benefits.

- Practical and logistical considerations.

10.   Case Studies and Commercial Successes

- Real examples of businesses and farms utilizing these techniques.

- Lessons learned and best practices.

11.   Environmental Impact and Sustainability

- Water usage and ecological footprint.

- Contribution to food security and urban agriculture.

12.   Automation and Technology in the Industry

1. Introduction to Hydroponics and Aquaponics

Definition and key differences:

Brief History and Development of Techniques: The idea of growing plants in nutrient solutions instead of soil can be traced back to experiments by botanists in the 19th century. However, it was only in the 20th century that hydroponics began to be seen as a practical solution to the challenge of growing food in hostile environments, such as desert areas or space environments. Aquaponics, though based on ancient principles of sustainable agriculture, gained popularity only in recent decades. The first modern aquaponic systems were developed in the 1970s and 1980s, often as university research projects. Since then, the technique has garnered increasing interest both as a hobby and a commercial practice. In conclusion, both hydroponics and aquaponics represent innovative approaches to agriculture that offer sustainable solutions to our planet's growing food needs. Both techniques continue to evolve, with new research and developments making them increasingly efficient and effective.

Advantages and Benefits: Hydroponic and aquaponic cultivation techniques offer several significant advantages compared to traditional agricultural methods.

1. **Water Efficiency:** Both techniques use much less water compared to conventional agriculture. This is particularly beneficial in regions where water is scarce.

2. **Total Growth Control:** Without the variability of soil, growers have direct control over the nutrients plants receive. This can lead to healthier plants and more abundant yields.

3. **Optimized Space:** Hydroponic and aquaponic cultivation can occur vertically, meaning more food can be produced in a smaller area, making it ideal for urban environments or areas with limited space.

4. **Reduced Diseases and Pests:** Since there's no soil, many common soil-borne diseases and pests are not a threat.

5. **Accelerated Plant Growth:** Under ideal conditions, plants can grow

faster as they have direct access to all the nutrients they need.

Definition of Systems and Equipment: There are several configurations and specific equipment used in both hydroponics and aquaponics. For instance, in hydroponics, there are nutrient film technique (NFT) systems, ebb and flow systems, aeroponics, and many others. Each has specific advantages, disadvantages, and logistical considerations. In aquaponics, considerations include the type of fish to use (tilapia and koi carp are common), as well as managing water pH and the balance between fish and plants. In both cases, adequate water circulation and appropriate lighting (natural or artificial) for the plants you want to grow are essential.

Sustainability and Environmental Impact: Hydroponics and aquaponics are often praised for their sustainability. By using fewer resources and producing less waste, both techniques can have a positive impact on the environment. For instance, aquaponics creates a closed ecosystem where water is recycled, reducing water consumption. Moreover, since there are no chemicals or pesticides involved, there's no harmful runoff that could pollute local waters. However, like any technology or practice, there are challenges. The energy needed for water pumping and treatment, artificial lighting if used, and other considerations can have an environmental impact. The key is to find a balance and use these techniques responsibly.

Integration of Hydroponics and Aquaponics: While hydroponics and aquaponics can function as separate systems, there's a growing interest in integrating the two techniques to leverage the strengths of both.

1. **Closed Loop and Efficiency:** By integrating hydroponics and aquaponics, it's possible to create a nearly self-sufficient cultivation

system. Fish produce waste that, once converted by beneficial bacteria, provides nutrients for plants. In turn, plants purify the water that's recycled back to the fish.

2. **Biodiversity:** Combining the two systems can lead to greater biodiversity in the created ecosystem. This can contribute to making the system more resilient to diseases and imbalances.

3. **Economic Yield:** While hydroponics can provide a bountiful plant harvest, aquaponics also offers a fish harvest. This diversification can increase income potential for farmers.

4. **Adaptability:** An integrated system can be adapted to fit various environmental conditions, from cold to tropical climates. This makes it ideal for a variety of geographical contexts.

Challenges in Integration: Despite the benefits, there are challenges in integrating hydroponics and aquaponics.

1. **Balancing Needs:** Plants and fish might have different needs in terms of pH, water temperature, and nutrient concentration. Balancing these needs can be complex.

2. **Initial Investment:** Setting up an integrated system might require a larger initial investment compared to creating a single hydroponic or aquaponic system.

3. **Disease Management:** If a disease affects one part of the system, like the fish, it can have repercussions on the plants and vice versa.

Future Perspectives: The integration of hydroponics and aquaponics represents a rapidly evolving field, with researchers, farmers, and entrepreneurs continuing to experiment and innovate. Potential applications range from large-scale food production to household and community gardens. With increasing awareness of environmental challenges and the need for sustainable food production, integrating these two methods could play a crucial role in the future of agriculture. In conclusion, both hydroponics and aquaponics, especially their integration, offer promising solutions to address some of the most urgent agricultural and environmental challenges of our time. Through further research and development, we may witness a revolution in how we grow and consume food.

Basic Principles of Hydroponics: Hydroponics is a form of agriculture in which plants are grown without soil, using mineral nutrient solutions in a soluble water medium. This technique offers the possibility of cultivating plants in environments where traditional soil is

unavailable or not ideal for cultivation.
How Hydroponics Works:

1. **Growing Medium:** Even though hydroponics doesn't use soil, plants still need a support for their roots. Common growing mediums include rock wool, perlite, vermiculite, and coconut coir. These mediums provide root support but not nutrients like soil does.

2. **Nutrient Solution:** Plants require nutrients to grow, and in a hydroponic system, these are supplied through a water-based nutrient solution. This solution contains all the essential macro and micronutrients that a plant needs to grow.

3. **Delivery Systems:** Various methods exist for delivering the nutrient solution to the plants, including drip

systems, flood and drain systems, the deep water culture (DWC) method, and many others. The choice of system depends on the environment, plant type, and grower preferences.

4. **Environmental Conditions:** Like in any form of cultivation, factors such as light, temperature, and humidity need to be monitored and controlled to ensure optimal plant growth.

Advantages of Hydroponics:

1. **Water Efficiency:** Hydroponics uses significantly less water compared to traditional soil-based cultivation.

2. **Faster Growth:** Due to the direct availability of nutrients, hydroponic plants tend to grow faster.

3. **Fewer Diseases and Pests:**
Without soil, many soil-borne pests
and diseases are eliminated.

4. **Limited Space Cultivation:**
Hydroponics is perfect for urban
environments and other places with
limited space.

5. **Total Control:** Growers have full
control over nutrients and pH,
enabling optimized cultivation.

Challenges of Hydroponics:

1. **Initial Cost:** Hydroponic equipment
can be expensive upfront, although it
might pay off over time with higher
yields.

2. **Complexity:** Unlike traditional
cultivation, hydroponics requires an

understanding and regular monitoring of nutrient solution, pH, etc.

3. **Technical Issues:** Like any system, hydroponics is prone to technical issues, such as broken pumps or malfunctioning lighting systems.

4. **Electricity Dependency:** Many hydroponic systems rely on electricity. Power outages could be a problem for the plants.

5. **Learning Curve:** Mastering the nuances of hydroponic cultivation can take time and experimentation.

Types of Hydroponic Systems:
Hydroponics isn't a single technique but an array of different methodologies, each with its specifics:

1. **Nutrient Film Technique (NFT):** In this system, a thin film of nutrient solution flows constantly along the roots of plants suspended in a channel. It's particularly suited for lightweight plants like lettuce.

2. **Aeroponics:** Plant roots are suspended in the air and regularly misted with nutrient solution. This provides ample oxygen to the roots, fostering rapid growth.

3. **Wick System:** One of the simplest methods, where a wick transports nutrient solution from the reservoir to the growing medium.

Monitoring and Management: The effectiveness of hydroponics relies on the grower's ability to monitor and manage the system:

1. **Nutrient Balance:** Too much or too little of a particular nutrient can harm plants. The ability to test and balance the nutrient solution is crucial.

2. **Oxygenation:** Plant roots require oxygen. Many hydroponic systems use aerators to ensure that roots receive the necessary oxygen.

3. **pH:** Correct pH is crucial to ensure plants can absorb nutrients. Most hydroponic plants thrive in a pH range of 5.5 to 6.5.

Sustainability and Environmental Impact: Hydroponics, when managed properly, can be a highly sustainable method of cultivation:

1. **Reduced Water Usage:** In a world where water becomes an increasingly precious resource, hydroponics can use up to 90% less water compared to traditional cultivation.

2. **No Erosion:** Since soil isn't used, there's no risk of erosion, a growing concern in many parts of the world.

3. **Less Waste:** The nutrient solution can be recycled and reused in many systems, reducing waste. Practical Considerations:

4. **Space:** While hydroponics can be practiced in small spaces, layout and organization are crucial. Each plant needs sufficient space to grow without impeding neighboring plants.

5. **Energy:** Although hydroponics can be more resource-efficient, it often requires energy sources for pumps, lights, and other systems.

Overall, hydroponics represents a promising advancement in modern agriculture. It offers innovative solutions to the growing challenges in agriculture and food supply. However, like any system, it requires attention, care, and a deep understanding to maximize its benefits.

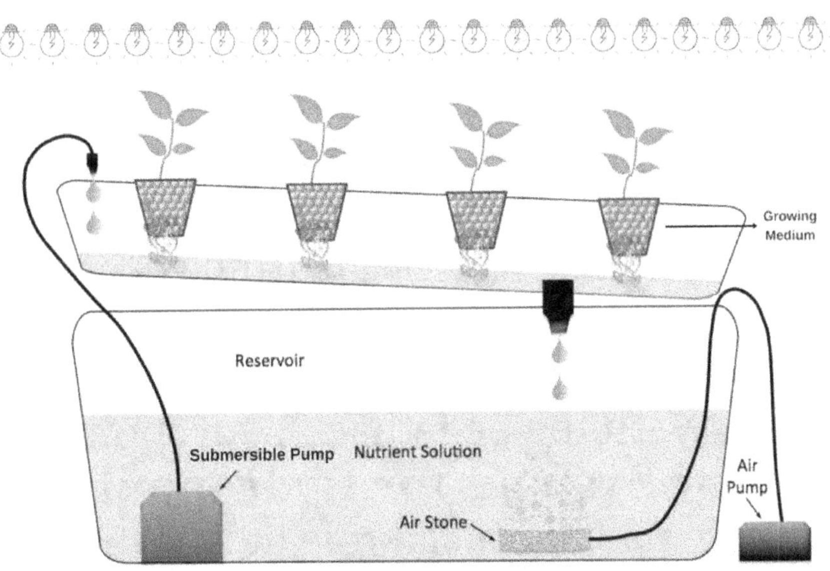

Selection of Growing Medium: Even though hydroponics eliminates the use of traditional soil, choosing the right growing medium is essential to support the plants:

1. **Rock Wool:** Made from the fusion of basalt and clay, rock wool is lightweight and provides good root support while allowing roots to breathe.
2. **Perlite:** This volcanic rock is heated until it expands into a lightweight and porous medium, perfect for oxygenation.
3. **Vermiculite:** It's a mineral similar to mica that's expanded through heat. It has a lightweight structure and can retain moisture, making it ideal for some hydroponic plants.
4. **Coconut Coir:** Made from coconut fibers, it's a completely natural medium that offers soil-like structure but with the benefits of hydroponics.

Lighting Systems for Hydroponics: Lighting plays a crucial role in hydroponics, especially in indoor operations:

1. **LED Lights:** With their energy efficiency and ability to produce specific light spectra, LED lights have become increasingly popular in hydroponics.
2. **High-Intensity Discharge (HID) Lights:** These lights produce a large amount of light and are often used for plants that require ample light, such as tomatoes.
3. **Fluorescent Lights:** While not as powerful as HID lights, fluorescent lights can be ideal for seedlings and low-light plants.

Disease and Pest Management: Without soil, many common pest threats are eliminated in hydroponics, but that doesn't mean it's immune:

1. **Nutrient Solutions:** Contaminated nutrient solution can quickly spread diseases to all plants in a hydroponic system. Monitoring and changing the solution regularly is essential.

2. **Airborne Pests:** Even without soil, pests like aphids and mites can infest plants. The use of natural insecticides and prevention are crucial.

Automation and Technology in Hydroponics: The advent of technology has taken hydroponics to a new level:

1. **pH and Nutrient Monitoring:** Devices exist that can constantly monitor and automatically adjust pH and nutrient levels in the solution.

2. **Irrigation Systems:** Automating irrigation through timers and sensors can ensure that plants receive the right amount of nutrient solution at the right time. Hydroponics, by combining traditional cultivation principles with advanced technology, offers revolutionary possibilities for future food production. However, like any advanced system, it requires deep knowledge and careful management to achieve optimal results.

Types of Hydroponic Systems: The versatility of hydroponics is reflected in the various types of systems available, each with unique characteristics:

1. **Drip System:** Uses a drip distribution mechanism to provide nutrient solution to plants. It's one of the most common methods and can be customized based on plant needs.
2. **Nutrient Film Technique (NFT) System:** In this system, a thin film of nutrient solution continuously flows over the roots of plants. It's particularly suitable for fast-growing plants like lettuce.
3. **Deep Water Culture (DWC) System:** Plants are suspended in a nutrient solution with roots submerged in water. Oxygenation is provided through porous stones diffusing bubbles into the solution.

Oxygenation and Aeration: Adequate oxygenation is crucial for ensuring plant health in a hydroponic system:

1. **Aeration Stones:** Used to introduce air bubbles into the nutrient solution, ensuring roots receive sufficient oxygen.

2. **Air Pumps:** Essential for maintaining aeration in systems like DWC, air pumps ensure a constant flow of air to the nutrient solution.

Climate Control: In indoor hydroponic cultivation, climate control can make a difference:

1. **Temperature Regulation:** Temperature can affect the growth rate of plants and the solution's oxygen retention ability. Using cooling or heating systems to maintain the optimal temperature is crucial.
2. **Humidity:** Excessive humidity can encourage mold and fungal growth. Using dehumidifiers or ventilation systems to control humidity is essential.

Nutritional Balancing: The nutrient solution is the heart of hydroponics, and its balance is crucial:

1. **Macro-Nutrients:** Nitrogen (N), Phosphorus (P), and Potassium (K) are the primary nutrients required in large quantities by plants. The right

combination, often referred to as the N-P-K ratio, varies based on the plant's growth stage.

2. **Micro-Nutrients:** Elements like Iron, Manganese, and Copper are required in small amounts but are essential for plant health.

Economic Aspects of Hydroponics:
Despite the advantages, there are also economic considerations:

1. **Initial Cost:** Setting up a hydroponic system can require a significant initial investment, especially if opting for an advanced system.

2. **Long-Term Savings:** While the initial investment might be high, the ability to grow year-round and increased yields can make hydroponics economically advantageous in the long run.

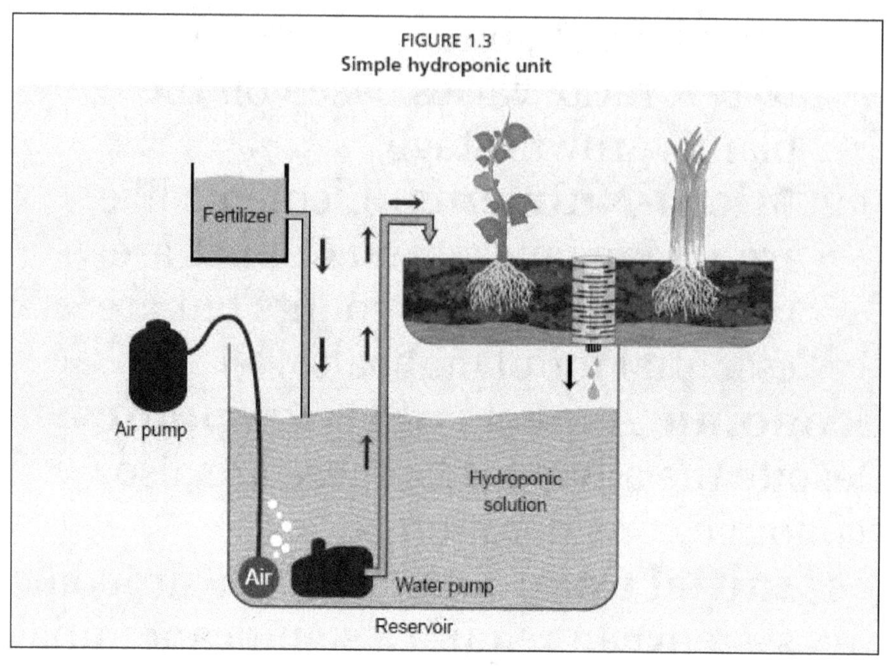

Principles of Aquaponics

Integration of Fish and Plants

Aquaponics is a unique combination of aquaculture (fish cultivation) and hydroponics (plant cultivation without soil). The basic idea is to use nutrient-rich water from fish tanks to nourish plants, and in return, plants filter and purify the water, which is then reintroduced into the aquatic system.

1. Nitrogen Cycle: One of the fundamental aspects of aquaponics is the nitrogen cycle. Fish produce waste, primarily ammonia. In aquaponics, bacteria convert this ammonia into nitrites and then into nitrates, which are used by plants as nutrients.

2. Continuous Flow vs. Flood and Drain Systems: There are various designs for aquaponic systems, but two of the most common are continuous flow, where water circulates continuously between the fish and plant systems, and flood and drain systems, which alternately fill and empty the grow beds.

Benefits of the Symbiotic Ecosystem
Aquaponics creates a symbiotic environment in which fish, plants, and

bacteria work together to establish a sustainable cultivation system.

1. Water Efficiency: Aquaponics uses significantly less water compared to traditional agriculture. Since water is continuously recycled within the system, the only losses occur due to evaporation and plant transpiration.

2. Waste Reduction: In an aquaponic system, what is waste for one component (like fish ammonia) becomes a resource for another (nitrates for plants). This efficient waste conversion and utilization reduce the need for external disposal.

3. Accelerated Plant Growth: With constant access to nutrient-rich and well-balanced elements, many plants have been observed to grow faster in aquaponic systems compared to traditional soil-based cultivation.

4. Sustainability: Not only does aquaponics decrease the need for water and chemical fertilizers, but it can also be set up as a near self-sustaining system, where fish food is grown within the same system or sourced sustainably.

5. Diverse Cultivation: While hydroponics often limits itself to fast-growing crops like lettuce and herbs, aquaponics can support a wider range of plants, including tomatoes, peppers, and cucumbers, due to the nutrient-rich solution provided by the fish.

In summary, aquaponics represents an innovative fusion of hydroponics and aquaculture. It offers a sustainable way of growing food, conserving precious resources, and providing a balanced and self-regulating ecosystem. Its growing popularity among urban farmers and gardening enthusiasts underscores the revolutionary potential of this cultivation method.

Ecosystem Dynamics in Aquaponics

1. Microbiology of Aquaponics:
Beyond fish and plants, a multitude of vital microorganisms populate an aquaponic system. These bacteria play a crucial role in converting fish waste into nutrients usable by plants. Bacteria like Nitrosomonas and Nitrobacter are essential for the nitrification process, converting ammonia into nitrites and then nitrates.

2. Oxygenation: To maintain optimal growth for fish and plants, water must be adequately oxygenated. Oxygen is essential not only for the fish but also for nitrifying bacteria. The use of aerators and pumps can ensure proper oxygen levels in the water.

Key Components of the System

While the basic principles of aquaponics are simple, practical implementation requires an understanding of the various key components of the system.

1. Fish Tanks: These are where fish live and produce waste that fuels the system. The size and design of the tank will influence the quantity and type of fish that can be raised.

2. Grow Beds: These are the areas where plants are cultivated. They can vary from deep grow beds suitable for larger plants like tomatoes and peppers to nutrient film technique (NFT) systems ideal for fast-growing plants like lettuce.

3. Solids and Filtration: Fish waste contains solid particles that can clog the system and create a harmful anaerobic environment. The use of settlers and filters can help remove these solid particles, keeping the water clean and promoting nitrification.

4. Control Systems: From monitoring pH to oxygenation, temperature, and light intensity, aquaponics requires constant supervision and potential adjustments. The implementation of sensors and automated control systems can facilitate this process, ensuring the environment remains optimal for both fish and plants.

Challenges of Aquaponics

Despite its many advantages, aquaponics also presents challenges:

1. Balance: Maintaining a balance between the number of fish and the quantity of plants is crucial. Too many fish can lead to an excess of nutrients, while too few fish might not provide enough nutrients for the plants.

2. Diseases: Just like in any agricultural system, diseases can pose a threat. The key is to prevent diseases through good management practices and, if necessary, treat diseases in ways that are safe for both fish and plants.

3. Initial Investment: Setting up an aquaponic system can require a significant initial investment, especially if high-quality components or automated control systems are used.

Role of Fish in Aquaponics

Fish are not just a food source in an aquaponic system; they are the engine that powers the entire ecosystem.

1. Types of Fish: While many might immediately think of carp or tilapia, numerous fish are suitable for aquaponics, including ornamental fish like goldfish and koi. The choice of fish will depend on factors like climate, system size, and the producer's goals (food production vs. aesthetics).

2. Feeding: Feeding fish plays a crucial role in producing nutrients for plants. While fish will convert some of the food they consume into body mass, most will be excreted as waste. The quality and quantity of food can directly influence the health of the aquaponic system.

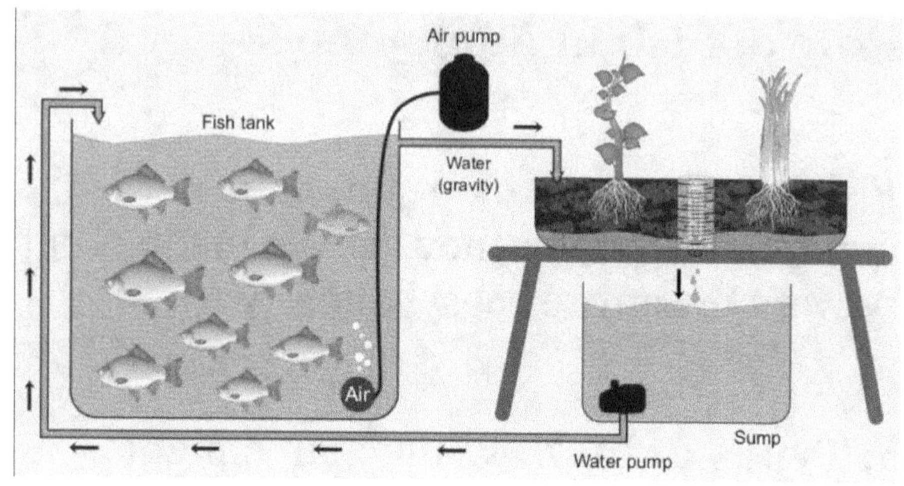

The Symbiosis of Fish and Plants

Aquaponics is based on the symbiotic relationship between fish and plants.

1. Nitrification Process: As discussed, fish waste, rich in ammonia, is converted by bacteria into nitrites and subsequently into nitrates. These nitrates are then absorbed by plants as the primary source of nitrogen, essential for their growth.

2. Water Purification: Plants not only absorb nutrients but also help filter the water, removing harmful substances and maintaining a healthy environment for the fish.

Economic Aspects of Aquaponics

Aquaponics offers not only environmental and agronomic benefits but also economic advantages.

1. Water Savings: Compared to traditional agriculture, an aquaponic system uses only a fraction of the water. This is particularly valuable in regions with limited water resources.

2. Dual Production: Producers can obtain both a vegetable harvest and a protein source (the fish) from the

same system, optimizing space and resources.

3. Growing Market: There is a growing demand for aquaponic products from environmentally conscious consumers interested in sustainability. This can offer premium prices to producers selling aquaponic products.

Design Considerations for Aquaponic Systems

1. Positioning: The location of an aquaponic system can have a significant impact on its efficiency. Considerations such as sun exposure, protection from strong winds, and proximity to resources like electricity are all crucial.

2. Scalability: While some aquaponic systems can be small and suitable for home use, others are large commercial operations. The ability to scale a system based on the producer's needs can influence the design and components used.

3. Aquaponics, with its combination of science, agriculture, and sustainability, represents a promising solution to address future agricultural challenges while providing healthy and sustainable food for growing populations.

4. Key Components and Equipment for Hydroponics and Aquaponics

Reservoir (Tank)

The reservoir, or tank, is essential for both systems, as it holds water and nutrients for plants (in hydroponics) and water and fish (in aquaponics).

1. Material: They are usually made of sturdy plastic or polyethylene, but they could also be constructed from metal or ceramic, depending on the size and specific requirements of the system.

2. Positioning: It should be placed in a location that avoids direct sunlight exposure, as this could overheat the water and damage both plants and fish.

Pumps

Water circulation is crucial for both systems, ensuring plants receive necessary nutrients and maintaining oxygenated water for the fish.

1. Submersible Pumps: These are the most common pumps used in hydroponic and aquaponic systems. They are immersed directly in the tank and are ideal for small to medium-sized systems.

2. Surface Pumps: Positioned outside the tank, these are suitable for larger setups or when you want to keep the heat generated by the pump away from the water.

Lights

Light is vital for plant photosynthesis. If a hydroponic or aquaponic system is located indoors or in a greenhouse, artificial lights may be necessary.

1. LED Lights: Extremely energy-efficient, LED lights are often used in modern hydroponic cultivation. They can be adjusted to emit specific wavelengths optimal for plant growth.

2. High-Intensity Discharge (HID) Lights: These lights offer very high intensity, ideal for specific stages of plant growth such as flowering.

Substrates

In hydroponic cultivation, substrates replace soil and provide mechanical support to plants.

1. Rockwool: This inert material is one of the most commonly used in hydroponics.

2. Expanded Clay: Lightweight and porous, these clay pellets are ideal for hydroponic cultivation and allow good air circulation around plant roots.

3. Perlite and Vermiculite: These expanded minerals are often used in substrate mixes.

Monitoring and Maintenance Tools

1. pH and EC Meters: Essential devices that help growers monitor and maintain appropriate levels of acidity and solute concentration in nutrient solutions.

2. Dissolved Oxygen: Particularly important for aquaponics, monitoring oxygen levels in the water is vital for fish health.

3. Thermometers: Maintaining the right water temperature is crucial for both plants and fish.

4. Cleaning Kit: Nets, tweezers, and brushes are essential for keeping various components of the system clean.

In conclusion, both hydroponics and aquaponics require accurate understanding and careful attention to components and equipment for successful operation. Each component has a key function in the system, and the absence of one can affect the efficiency of the entire ecosystem.

Filters

In aquaponics, filters are crucial for removing suspended solids, such as fish waste, and maintaining clean water for plants.

1. Mechanical Filters: These remove particles and debris from the water through a physical mechanism. They may use sponges, foams, or other materials.

2. Biological Filters: These utilize beneficial microorganisms to break down organic waste, converting it into compounds useful for plants.

Heaters and Chillers

Maintaining a stable water temperature is essential for both plants and fish.

1. Heaters: These are used to maintain the water at an ideal temperature, especially during winter months or in cold environments.

2. Chillers: In warm climates or seasons, it might be necessary to cool the water to ensure an optimal environment for fish and plants.

Aerators

Essential for providing oxygen to plant roots and fish water.

1. Porous Stones: These are placed in the water and connected to a pump that provides air. They release small bubbles that oxygenate the water.

2. Surface Ventilators: These can be used in large tanks to increase water circulation and oxygenation.

Support Systems

Particularly relevant in hydroponics, these systems support plants since they don't use traditional soil.

1. Nets: Provide physical support to plants, especially those with heavy fruits like tomatoes or cucumbers.

2. Vertical Structures: Allow plants to be cultivated in limited spaces, utilizing height rather than horizontal extension.

Nutrient Solutions and Supplements

In hydroponics, the nutrient solution provides plants with all necessary minerals.

1. Macronutrients: Such as nitrogen, phosphorus, and potassium, are essential for plant growth.

2. Micronutrients: Like iron, manganese, and zinc, are required in smaller quantities but are still vital.

3. pH Up and Down: Chemical products used to regulate the pH of the nutrient solution, ensuring it remains in the ideal range for nutrient absorption.

Advanced Monitoring Systems

With the advent of technology, increasingly sophisticated tools are available.

1. Automatic Control Systems: These devices can monitor and automatically adjust various parameters like pH, temperature, and nutrient levels.

2. Cameras and Sensors: These can be used to remotely monitor plants and detect issues such as diseases or pests.

In summary, the proper choice and management of equipment are crucial for the success of any hydroponic or aquaponic system. Each component has a specific role and, if well cared for, can ensure optimal plant growth and good fish health. With the ongoing evolution of technology, growers now have access to more advanced tools that can further simplify and optimize the process.

5. Popular Hydroponic Systems

DWC (Deep Water Culture)

Description: The DWC system, also known as deep water culture, is a technique where plants are suspended in a nutrient solution, with roots immersed directly in water. Oxygen is supplied to the roots through aerators that create bubbles in the water, ensuring roots receive sufficient oxygen.

Advantages: • Rapid Growth: With constant access to nutrients and oxygen, plants grow faster.

• Simplicity: DWC systems are relatively simple to set up and manage.

• Lower Initial Costs: Compared to some other systems, DWC can have lower initial costs.

Disadvantages:

• Disease Risk: Since all plants share the same nutrient and water, a diseased plant can quickly spread the disease to others.

• Water Maintenance: pH and nutrient levels need to be regularly monitored and adjusted.

• Energy Consumption: Aeration systems must run constantly to provide oxygen to the roots.

NFT (Nutrient Film Technique)

Description: In the NFT system, a thin nutrient solution is constantly circulated over a thin layer (film) on which plant roots rest. Plants are suspended in net pots that allow roots to come into contact with the flowing nutrient solution.

Advantages:

• Efficient Water Use: As water is recirculated, the NFT system is very water-efficient.

• Oxygenation: Roots exposed to the nutrient film also receive ample oxygen from the air.

• Flexibility: The setup can be configured in various shapes and sizes based on available space.

Disadvantages:

• Vulnerability to Power Failures: If the pump shuts down, roots can dry out quickly as they're not immersed in water like in DWC.

• Complexity: Flow regulation and general maintenance may require special attention.

• Disease Risk: Similar to DWC, diseases can spread quickly through the nutrient solution.

Other Hydroponic Systems:

• Ebb & Flow System: Plants are periodically flooded with a nutrient solution, which is then drained, allowing roots to breathe.

• Drip System: The nutrient solution is delivered directly to plant roots through drippers.

• Aeroponics: Roots are suspended in the air and misted with a nutrient solution.

Each hydroponic system has its own advantages and challenges, so the choice depends on the grower's specific goals, available resources, and the particular needs of the plants they intend to cultivate.

Ebb & Flow System

Description: Also known as the "flood and drain" system, the Ebb & Flow system operates by periodically filling the growing tray with a nutrient solution and then completely draining it. Plants are planted in pots or containers filled with an inert medium such as perlite or expanded clay.

Advantages: • Excellent root aeration: After each flooding cycle, roots receive abundant oxygen from the air. •

Adaptability: Can be easily adjusted to spaces of different sizes and shapes.

• Reduced risk of diseases: The nutrient solution does not remain in contact with the roots for extended periods, reducing the risk of diseases like root rot.

Disadvantages:

• Energy consumption: The pump required to fill and empty the reservoir can consume more energy compared to other systems.

• Complexity: The system requires proper timing to ensure that plants receive enough nutrients without drowning the roots.

• Initial cost: May require a higher initial investment due to the pumps and timers needed.

Drip System

Description: In this system, the nutrient solution is directly provided to the plant roots through drip emitters. Each plant has its own irrigation system, allowing customization of the amount of nutrition each plant receives.

Advantages: • Precision: Allows each plant to receive exactly the amount of nutrient solution it needs.

• Water efficiency: Minimizes water wastage.

• Versatility: Suitable for cultivations of various sizes, from small home gardens to large commercial greenhouses.

Disadvantages: • Maintenance: Drip emitters can become clogged and require regular cleaning. • Installation: The setup can be more complex compared to other systems. • Cost: The drip system and related equipment can be costly.

Aeroponic System

Description: In aeroponics, plant roots are suspended in air and are periodically misted with a nutrient solution. This system provides plants with an excellent combination of nutrients and oxygen.

Advantages:

• Rapid growth: Direct access to both nutrients and oxygen promotes rapid plant growth.

• Water savings: Aeroponics uses much less water compared to traditional cultivation methods.

• Minimal disease risk: The absence of a substrate reduces the risk of soil-borne diseases.

Disadvantages:

• Technological complexity: Aeroponics requires sophisticated technology to mist the solution and maintain the correct environment.

• High energy consumption: Pumps and misters need to operate regularly.

• Initial investment: Due to the need for specialized equipment, the initial investment can be higher compared to other hydroponic systems.

In conclusion, the choice of the most suitable hydroponic system depends on various factors, including budget, available space, types of plants to be grown, and the grower's level of experience. While some systems are ideal for beginners, others may require more experience and attention to detail. Nevertheless, with proper planning and maintenance, hydroponic cultivation can offer impressive yields in terms of plant growth and production.

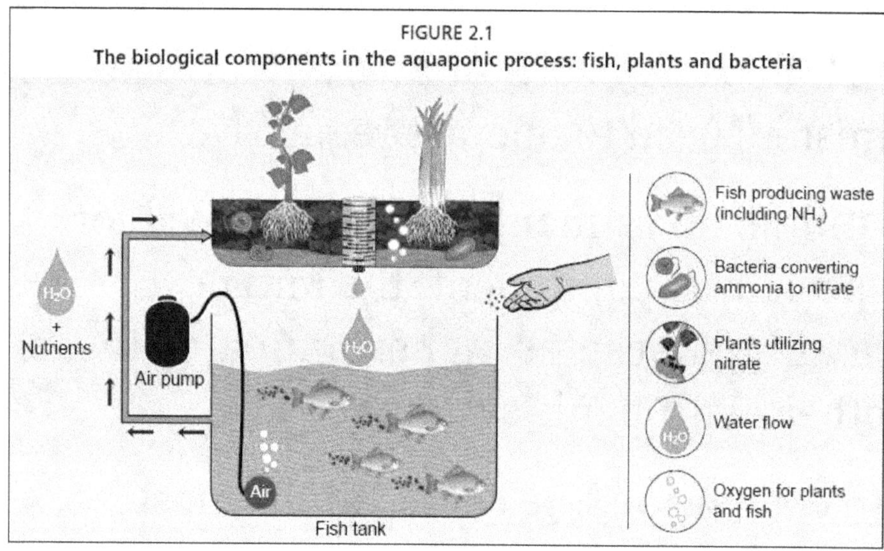

6.Configuring an Aquaponic System

Choosing Fish and Plants Fish for Aquaponics

1. Tilapia: One of the most popular fish for aquaponics. They are hardy, grow quickly, and tolerate various water conditions. They are also a good choice for those who want fish both for food production and for aquaponics.

2. Koi Carp: Not typically used for consumption, but an excellent choice for combining visual beauty with functionality. Koi help produce the necessary nutrients for plants but are primarily ornamental.

3. Perch: Thrive in aquaponic systems and are in high demand as edible fish.

4. Barbs: Although not as common as tilapia or perch, they are a good choice for smaller systems or those looking for variety.

5. Freshwater Shrimp: Offer an interesting variation from traditional fish and are also delicious to eat.

Plant Selection Certain plants thrive particularly well in aquaponic systems due to the nutritional richness provided by fish-enriched water. Here are some common plant choices:

1. Lettuce: Grows quickly and requires fewer nutrients compared to other plants.

2. Spinach: A fast-growing vegetable that benefits from a constant supply of nutrients.

3. Basil and Other Herbs: Grow extremely well and can be continuously harvested.

4. Tomatoes: While they require a well-balanced system, they can yield abundant harvests.

5. Peppers: Like tomatoes, they thrive in a well-balanced system.

6. Strawberries: Can be grown in an NFT (Nutrient Film Technique) system or on floating grow beds.

Ecosystem Balance

1. Nitrogen Cycle: In an aquaponic system, balancing the nitrogen cycle is crucial. Fish waste, primarily ammonia, is converted into nitrites and then nitrates by beneficial bacteria. These nitrates serve as nutrients for the plants.

2. Oxygenation: Providing adequate oxygen to both fish and plant roots is essential. Pumps and diffusers are often used to ensure well-oxygenated water.

3. pH: Water pH affects plants' ability to absorb nutrients. Most plants prefer a pH of 5.5-7.0. Monitoring and adjusting pH regularly may be necessary.

4. Temperature: While plants and fish have slightly different temperature requirements, it's essential to keep the water within a temperature range acceptable to both.

5. Disease and Pest Control: Avoid using chemical pesticides, as they could harm or kill the fish. Instead, opt for biological control methods or natural solutions.

6. Fish Density: Too many fish could lead to excess waste and insufficient oxygen, while too few fish may not provide enough nutrients for the plants.

7. Fish Feeding: Using high-quality fish food helps reduce unwanted waste in the system and ensures healthy and productive fish.

Monitoring and Regulation

1. Water Testing: Regular monitoring of water parameters like ammonia, nitrites, nitrates, pH, and dissolved oxygen is crucial. Test kits are available, making this process relatively simple even for beginners.

2. Buffer Solutions: Adjusting water pH might require the addition of buffer solutions, both acidic and alkaline, to maintain pH at an ideal level for plants and fish.

3. Alarm Systems: With modern technology, alarm systems can be

installed to notify farmers of power outages, pump malfunctions, or drastic pH or temperature variations.

Extension and Scalability The beauty of aquaponics lies in its scalability. You can start with a small home-based system and later expand to large commercial setups.

1. Modular Systems: For those looking to expand their aquaponic setup, adopting a modular approach can be advantageous. This allows adding new modules without disturbing the existing system.

2. Automation: With the advent of the Internet of Things (IoT) and smart technology, much of the monitoring and maintenance of an aquaponic system can now be automated, reducing manual labor and human errors.

Sustainability and Water Saving Aquaponics, being a closed-loop system, consumes significantly less water compared to traditional farming. Water is continuously recycled between the fish tanks and plant grow beds.

1. Efficient Water Use: Aquaponics is estimated to use only 10% of the water required by traditional soil-based farming.

2. Reduced Wastage: Since water is recycled, there are no significant losses due to evaporation or drainage. Additionally, there's no need for chemical fertilizers, which often cause pollution in conventional agriculture runoff.

Conclusion on Aquaponic System Configuration Setting up an aquaponic system requires in-depth understanding and detailed planning, but the benefits in terms of sustainable food production, water saving, and waste reduction make this cultivation method highly effective and environmentally responsible. With careful attention to fish and plant selection, ecosystem balance, and maintenance, aquaponics can offer a revolutionary agricultural solution for the future.

7. Nutrition and pH: Crucial Factors for Growth Optimal plant growth in hydroponic and aquaponic systems requires careful management of nutrients and pH. These two factors are intrinsically related, and fluctuations in one can directly impact the other, influencing plant health and, in the case of aquaponics, fish health as well.

Balancing Nutrients in Hydroponic and Aquaponic Systems

1. Hydroponic Systems: • Nutrient
   Solutions: Success in hydroponics
   hinges on the correct formulation of
   the nutrient solution. This solution
   contains all essential macro and
   micronutrients that plants need to
   grow. Different commercially
   available formulations exist, but
   customized blends can also be
   prepared based on specific plant
   requirements. • Regular Monitoring:
   It's essential to regularly check the
   nutrient concentration in the
   hydroponic solution. Tools like
   conductivity meters can help
   determine salt concentration in the
   solution and, consequently, its
   nutritional content.

2. Aquaponic Systems: • Nutrient Supply
   from Fish: The primary source of
   nutrients in an aquaponic system
   comes from fish waste. These waste

products, rich in nitrogen, are converted by beneficial bacteria into nitrates that plants can absorb. • Supplements: Even though fish provide many essential nutrients, you might need to add supplements, especially for micronutrients like iron that may not be present in sufficient quantities.

Importance of pH Monitoring • Some nutrients become more soluble and, therefore, more available to plants within certain pH ranges. For example, iron tends to be more available in a slightly acidic environment.

2. Hydroponic Systems: • pH Control: In hydroponics, pH control is essential to ensure that plants have consistent access to nutrients. As plants absorb nutrients, they can alter the pH of the nutrient solution. Hence, periodically

monitoring and adjusting pH is crucial. Usually, a pH range of 5.5 to 6.5 is considered ideal for most plants grown in hydroponic systems. • pH Adjusters: Specific commercial products exist to increase or decrease the pH of the nutrient solution. Using products specially formulated for hydroponics is essential to avoid unwanted contamination.

3. Aquaponic Systems: • Balance Between Plants and Fish: While plants might prefer a slightly acidic pH, fish require a more neutral pH to thrive. Therefore, finding a balance is important, usually maintaining pH between 6.8 and 7.2. • Stability: Rapid and significant pH fluctuations can be harmful to both plants and fish. Thus, daily monitoring and gradual adjustment are essential. The use of

buffers can help maintain stable pH levels.

Nutrition and pH play a crucial role in the success of any hydroponic or aquaponic system. A thorough understanding of how to balance these factors will ensure optimal plant growth and fish health. As with any farming system, the key is continuous observation and adaptation based on the needs of the plants and animals in the system.

Meticulous management of nutrition and pH is essential to ensure lush and healthy plant growth in any cultivation system. Within the realm of hydroponics and aquaponics, these two components play an even more crucial role, given that plants depend entirely on the provided nutrient solution.

1.

Essential Nutrients:
  - **Macroelements:** These are nutrients required in large quantities. They include nitrogen (N), phosphorus (P), potassium (K), calcium (Ca), magnesium (Mg), and sulfur (S). Each of these plays a fundamental role in the plant's life cycle. For example, nitrogen is crucial for leaf growth, while potassium is essential for flowering and fruiting.
  - **Microelements:** These are needed in smaller amounts but are still essential. They comprise iron (Fe), manganese (Mn), boron (B), molybdenum (Mo), zinc (Zn), copper (Cu), and chlorine (Cl). Although present in traces, their deficiency can cause evident problems like leaf chlorosis or deformation.

2. **Nutrient Sources:**
  - **Hydroponics:** Nutrients are supplied directly to the plant

through a nutrient solution. This solution is a balanced mixture of macro and microelements dissolved in water. The composition may vary depending on the plant type and its growth stage.

- **Aquaponics:** Nutrients primarily come from fish waste. While nitrogen is abundantly supplied in the form of ammonia from the fish, other nutrients might be lacking and require supplementation.

3. **Importance of pH:**

- **pH:** pH can significantly affect the plant's ability to absorb nutrients. If pH is too high or too low, certain nutrients can become less available, causing nutritional deficiencies even if they are present in the solution.

- **Ideal pH:** The ideal pH varies depending on the plants, but in most hydroponic and aquaponic systems, a range between 5.5 and

7.5 is generally considered optimal.

4. **Regulation and Monitoring:**
   - **Constant Monitoring:** It's crucial to constantly monitor the solution to ensure that pH and nutrient concentration are within desired ranges.
   - **Hydroponics:** The nutrient solution might require frequent adjustments, while in aquaponics, the self-regulating ecosystem might require fewer interventions but more attentive monitoring to prevent imbalances.

5. **Interactions and Balancing:**
   - **Interactions:** It's not just about providing nutrients; understanding how they interact is crucial. For instance, an excess of a particular nutrient can inhibit the absorption of another.
   - **Aquaponics:** Balancing fish health and plant nutrition is crucial in aquaponics. An excess

of nutrients might benefit plants but harm fish.

6. **Challenges and Solutions:**

- **pH and Nutrient Management:** Managing pH and nutrients presents challenges. For example, tap water might have a high pH or chlorine, which can harm plants. Using distilled or filtered water can help mitigate these issues.

- **Nutrient Integration:** In aquaponics, you might need to supplement with nutrients not adequately provided by fish waste. This could include iron, calcium, or potassium. In conclusion, nutrition and pH are two pillars of cultivation in both hydroponics and aquaponics. A deep understanding and the ability to balance and regulate these factors can make the difference between a thriving harvest and growth issues.

...

8. **Management of Pests and Diseases** Managing pests and diseases is one of the main challenges in plant cultivation, regardless of the adopted system. In hydroponic and aquaponic techniques, the absence of soil presents both advantages and disadvantages in terms of pest and disease control. Prevention is key, but when infestations occur, rapid intervention with effective and preferably sustainable solutions is essential.

1. **Advantages of Soilless Cultivation:**
   - **Reduction of Soil Pests:** Many pathogens and parasites reside and multiply in the soil. Hydroponic and aquaponic cultivation eliminates this primary source of infestation.
   - **Controlled Environment:** Cultivating in a controlled environment (such as greenhouses) allows more

targeted management and limits the access of many external pests.

2. **Specific Challenges:**
   - **Rapid Spread:** In hydroponic systems, in particular, a pathogen or parasite can spread quickly through the nutrient solution, infecting the entire system rapidly.
   - **Treatment Limitations:** In aquaponics, the use of many chemical pesticides is prohibited as they could harm or kill the fish.
3. **Prevention:**
   - **Hygiene:** Keeping the cultivation area clean is essential. This includes regular sterilization of equipment and the removal of dead or diseased plants.
   - **Isolation:** Introduce new plants only after quarantining them and

ensuring the absence of parasites.

- **Monitoring:** Regular checks allow for early detection and management of any infestations.

4. **Organic and Sustainable Approaches:**

- **Beneficial Insects:** Using natural predators like ladybugs or predatory mites can help control pests like aphids and mites.
- **Essential Oils:** Oils like neem oil have repellent properties and can be used as preventive treatments.
- **Biological Solutions:** Beneficial bacteria like Bacillus thuringiensis can be used to manage specific insect infestations.
- **Altering Conditions:** Changing environmental conditions such as temperature or humidity can

create a less hospitable environment for certain pests.

5. **Physical Treatments:**
   - **Physical Barriers:** Using nets or screens can prevent access to many flying pests.
   - **Manual Removal:** In the case of minor infestations, manual removal (as with aphids) can be effective.
6. **Research and Innovation:**
   - **With the increasing popularity of hydroponics and aquaponics, research is focusing on new methods to prevent and treat pests and diseases in these systems. Harnessing these new discoveries can provide increasingly effective and sustainable solutions.

The challenge of maintaining a disease and pest-free environment in hydroponic and aquaponic systems is constant and requires a deep understanding of the dynamics of these ecosystems. Here are further details and insights into pest and disease management in these systems:

7. **Microbiome and Plant Health:**
    - **Beneficial Flora:** Just as our gut has a microbiome that aids digestion, plant roots host a range of beneficial microorganisms. In hydroponic and aquaponic systems, it's possible to cultivate beneficial microbial flora that helps combat pathogens and parasites.
    - **Plant Probiotics:** There are products on the market designed to improve the root microbiome, enhancing natural defenses against diseases and pests.
8. **Water Analysis:**
    - **Waterborne Pathogens:** Water can carry various pathogens. It's essential to

test and treat the water to prevent disease spread.

- **Water Treatments:** In addition to filtration, UV sterilization is an effective method to eliminate pathogens from water without using chemicals.

7. **Environment and Design:**
   - **Air Flow:** Adequate air circulation prevents the accumulation of humidity and the settlement of pathogens like mold. Investing in good ventilation systems is crucial.
   - **Plant Placement:** Avoid overcrowding of plants. Ensuring sufficient space between plants helps prevent the spread of diseases and pests.

8. **Training and Education:**
   - **Understanding Pests:** Being able to quickly identify common and rare pests allows for timely

intervention. Continuous training is therefore essential.

- **Workshops and Courses:** Participating in hydroponic and aquaponic agriculture workshops, courses, and seminars can provide updated insights on managing and preventing pests and diseases.

9. **Support Networks and Community:**
    - **Groups and Forums:** Joining grower groups or forums can be an effective way to share experiences, challenges, and solutions related to pest and disease management.
    - **Cooperation:** Collaborating with other growers and research institutions can expedite the discovery of new solutions and strategies.

10. **Ongoing Review:**
    - **Post-Cultivation Analysis:** At the end of each growing cycle, it's essential to examine and record

any issues related to pests and diseases to make improvements in the next cycle.

- **Practices Update:** Research and innovations in this field are continually evolving. It's important to stay updated and be prepared to modify and adapt farming practices accordingly.

The management of pests and diseases in hydroponic and aquaponic systems is a combination of prevention, timely intervention, and continuous learning. The key to success lies in being proactive, staying informed, and leveraging available resources and innovations.

...

9. **Integration of Hydroponics and Aquaponics:** The integration of hydroponics and aquaponics represents an exciting frontier in sustainable agriculture, combining the best of both worlds to achieve optimal results. A hybrid system can offer the benefits of highly controllable hydroponics alongside the sustainable

ecology of aquaponics. Here's how such integration could be realized:

Creating Hybrid Systems to Maximize Benefits:

1. **Dual Production:** The main attraction of integration is the ability to produce both crops and animal protein (fish) in the same system, optimizing space and resources.

2. **Resource Optimization:** Water used for fish farming can be purified by plants, which, in turn, benefit from the nutrients provided by fish waste, creating a closed cycle of nutrient consumption and production.

3. **Risk Diversification:** Having both hydroponic and aquaponic components allows farmers to diversify risk. If one component were to fail, the other could still produce.

Practical and Logistic Considerations:

4. **System Design:** Designing an integrated system requires a deep understanding of both approaches. For example, the configuration of growing beds, fish tanks, pumps, and other components must be synchronized to work in harmony.
5. **Nutrient Balancing:** While plants can benefit from nutrients from fish waste, additional nutrient supplementation might be necessary for particularly demanding crops.
6. **Disease Control:** An integrated system might be exposed to pathogens from both aquaponics and hydroponics. Accurate management and monitoring are essential.
7. **Maintenance:** Although an integrated system can offer resource efficiency benefits, it

might require more maintenance than separate systems. For instance, a malfunctioning pump could affect both plants and fish.

8. **Training and Education:** Given the complexity of hybrid systems, continuous training is fundamental. Operators must be able to understand and manage the unique challenges posed by the integration of hydroponics and aquaponics.

In-depth Exploration of Hydroponics and Aquaponics Integration: As the agricultural sector seeks increasingly efficient and sustainable ways to produce food, the integration of hydroponics and aquaponics emerges as a promising solution. Harmonizing these two cultivation methods presents new challenges, but also significant opportunities. Let's delve deeper:

Energy Efficiency:

- **Resource Sharing:** Using a single system for fish rearing and plant cultivation allows for sharing resources such as water and energy, reducing operational costs. For example, lights used for plant growth can also serve as a source of heat for fish tanks in certain climates.

- **Reduced Ecological Footprint:** Through water recycling between plant and animal components, water usage is significantly reduced, making integrated systems particularly suitable for areas with limited water resources.

Economic Aspects:

- **Income Diversification:** Having both crops and fish offers farmers the opportunity to diversify their income sources. While the vegetable market might be saturated, there might be demand for specific fish species.
- **Initial Costs:** Establishing a hybrid system might have higher initial costs compared to single systems. However, long-term benefits in terms of resource savings and efficiency could offset these costs.

Ecological Aspects:

- **Sustainability:** Besides lower water consumption, integrated systems can help reduce waste production. Fish waste becomes natural fertilizer for plants, eliminating the need for chemical fertilizers.
- **Biodiversity:** When managed correctly, these systems can support a wide range of plant and animal species, promoting biodiversity both above and below the water's surface.

Technology and Innovation:
- **Monitoring and Automation:** With the advent of Internet of Things (IoT) technologies, it's possible to monitor and control various system parameters in real-time, such as pH, temperature, and nutrient levels. This automation can help maintain balance in the system.
- **Research and Development:** While hydroponics and aquaponics are well-established practices, the integration of the two is a relatively

new field that offers ample opportunities for research and innovation.

In summary, the integration of hydroponics and aquaponics represents an evolution in sustainable food production. Despite challenges, with the right knowledge, technology, and management, these hybrid systems can revolutionize how we think about the agriculture of the future.

Case Studies and Commercial Successes: Hydroponics and aquaponics are becoming increasingly popular not only among hobbyists but also among commercial growers. This is due to the numerous advantages these systems offer, such as increasing resource efficiency and the ability to cultivate in areas with poor or non-existent soil. Here are some case studies of companies and farms that have successfully leveraged these techniques:

1. **Green Sky Growers, Florida, USA:**

- **Story:** Located on the rooftop of a building in Winter Garden, Florida, Green Sky Growers is a hydroponic and aquaponic greenhouse that produces fish and vegetables in an integrated system.
- **Lessons Learned:** The integrated system saves water and reduces waste. The rooftop location demonstrates that urban farming can be productive and sustainable.

2. **Sundrop Farms, South Australia:**
   - **Story:** This company revolutionized hydroponic cultivation by using concentrated solar energy to provide power and desalinate seawater for irrigation.
   - **Lessons Learned:** Through technological innovation, it's possible to grow in extreme conditions, such as the arid areas of Australia, using renewable resources.

3. **The Plant, Chicago, USA:**
   - **Story:** A former sausage factory transformed into a hub of sustainable food production. Inside, aquaponics plays a key role in fish and vegetable production, while the building's organic waste powers an anaerobic digester that provides energy.
   - **Lessons Learned:** Recycling and symbiosis can be taken to new levels in an urban environment, demonstrating that food can be produced locally and sustainably even in large cities.

4.

Aquaponics UK, United Kingdom:

   - **Story:** A non-profit organization dedicated to aquaponics research and education. They have worked on various projects, from the UK to Nepal, integrating aquaponics with other forms of food production.

- **Lessons Learned:** Aquaponics is not only for developed countries. It can have a significant impact even in areas with limited resources, providing food and creating economic opportunities.

5. **GrowUp Urban Farms, London, United Kingdom:**

- **Story:** Located in the heart of London, GrowUp Urban Farms is the city's first commercial aquaponic facility. It produces salads and fish in a controlled environment, providing fresh and local food to residents.

- **Lessons Learned:** Urban farming can significantly reduce the carbon footprint of food by eliminating the need for long-distance transportation.

These case studies are just the tip of the iceberg when it comes to successes in hydroponics and aquaponics. With a growing focus on sustainability and efficiency in food production, we are likely to see many more examples emerge in the future. Each company or farm has its unique challenges, but what they have in common is the demonstration that with innovation and determination, sustainable agriculture can thrive.

The combination of hydroponics and aquaponics has the potential to revolutionize how we view agriculture, particularly in areas with limited water resources or unsuitable soils. By further examining case studies and successes, we can better understand how these techniques are changing the global agricultural landscape.

6. **Edenworks, Brooklyn, New York:**

   - **Story:** Edenworks is an urban farm that cultivates both fish and vegetables under the same roof, using water from the aquaculture system to nourish the plants, and in turn, the plants clean the water for the fish.

   - **Lessons Learned:** Urban agriculture can provide fresh food to urban communities, as well as create jobs and education on sustainability.

7. **Sweet Water Organics, Milwaukee, USA:**

- **Story:** This enterprise transformed an abandoned warehouse into an urban farm, producing fish and vegetables and demonstrating that aquaponics can regenerate declining industrial communities.

- **Lessons Learned:** Abandoned spaces can be repurposed in innovative ways, providing not only food but also community and economic regeneration.

8. **ECF Farmsystems, Berlin, Germany:**

- **Story:** Situated in Berlin, ECF Farmsystems is a leading example of how aquaponics can be implemented in a European urban setting, producing fresh fish and vegetables for the local population.

- **Lessons Learned:** The adaptability of aquaponics means it can be applied in a variety of climates and contexts, from warm countries to cold urban environments.

9. **The Aquaponics Lab, UK:**

- **Story:** This research project focuses on spreading aquaponics as a means to address food security and environmental issues. They provide training, resources, and support to the aquaponic community.

- **Lessons Learned:** Education is crucial. Raising awareness and educating people about aquaponics can lead to greater

adoption and innovation in the
industry.

10. **SAIT Polytechnic's Green Building Technologies Lab, Canada:**

- **Story:** SAIT is exploring how to integrate aquaponics into green building systems, aiming to create buildings that are not only energy-efficient but also produce food.

- **Lessons Learned:** The fusion of technologies can lead to entirely new solutions. The buildings of the future might not only provide shelter but also food, creating a truly sustainable environment.

As we examine these case studies, it's evident that hydroponics and aquaponics are becoming increasingly significant in a variety of contexts, from commercial to educational. With growing concerns about food security, water supply, and sustainability, the combination of hydroponics and aquaponics offers innovative and promising solutions to address some of the biggest challenges of our time.

Environmental Impact and Sustainability: A New Era in Agriculture: Hydroponics and aquaponics have often been praised for their potential in terms of sustainability and lower environmental impact compared to traditional agriculture. Let's examine these aspects in detail:

Water Usage:

1. **Water Efficiency:** Hydroponic and aquaponic techniques use significantly less water compared to traditional agriculture. While conventional agriculture can lose a large amount of water due to

evaporation and runoff, closed systems like hydroponics and aquaponics recycle and reuse water, reducing the overall amount needed.

2. **Reduced Water Waste:** Excess water is collected and re-fed into the system, leading to minimal waste. This is particularly advantageous in water-scarce areas.

Ecological Impact:

1. **Reduced Pesticide Use:** In a controlled environment like hydroponics or aquaponics, managing and preventing infestations is easier, reducing the need for chemical pesticides.

2. **Less Soil Erosion:** Since these methods don't use soil, they eliminate issues like erosion, contributing to preserving soil and groundwater quality.

Contribution to Food Security:

1. **Consistent Production:**
   Hydroponic and aquaponic systems
   can produce food year-round,
   regardless of external weather
   conditions. This can help mitigate
   food security issues in areas with
   short growing seasons or
   unpredictable climates.

Farming in Limited Spaces:

- **Vertical Farming:** Hydroponic and
  aquaponic systems are often utilized
  in vertical farming projects, where
  plants are grown on stacked layers or
  shelves. This maximizes production in
  confined spaces, such as urban
  buildings or greenhouses.

- **Geographic Flexibility:** The ability
  to grow food in confined or
  unconventional spaces, like rooftops
  or indoor areas, means fresh produce

can be produced closer to consumers, even in densely populated urban areas.

Contribution to Urban Agriculture:

- **Local Access:** Urban agriculture reduces the need to transport food over long distances, resulting in fresher food and reduced energy used in transportation.

- **Education:** The visibility of urban agriculture provides educational opportunities for the community. People can learn directly about sustainable farming practices and the value of locally produced food.

Reduced Carbon Footprint:

- **Less Transportation:** Local food production means less transportation and, consequently, a decrease in greenhouse gas emissions.

- **Clean Energy:** Many hydroponic and aquaponic systems use renewable energy sources like solar power to fuel their operations, further reducing their carbon footprint.

In summary, hydroponics and aquaponics not only offer innovative methods of food production but also carry profound implications for sustainability, the environment, and our relationship with food. While these techniques are not without challenges, their potential in terms of reducing environmental impact and contributing to food security is undeniable. In the context of a growing global population and climate challenges, these methods represent an essential part of the future of agriculture.

Environmental Impact and Sustainability in Hydroponics and Aquaponics:

1. **Water Efficiency:** Hydroponics and aquaponics are remarkably water-efficient compared to traditional agriculture. Under optimal conditions, aquaponics can use up to 90% less water than traditional soil-based cultivation. This is because water is continuously recycled through the system, with minimal losses due to evaporation and percolation.

2. **Pesticide Elimination:** Many hydroponic and aquaponic systems use little to no pesticides compared to traditional agriculture. This reduces consumers' exposure to chemical residues and decreases the environmental impact associated with

the use and production of these compounds.

3. **Reduced Agricultural Runoff:** Agricultural runoff, rich in fertilizers and other chemicals, can lead to eutrophication of rivers and lakes, causing harmful algal blooms and creating "dead zones" in water bodies. Properly managed hydroponic and aquaponic systems do not produce such runoff, as nutrients are contained and recycled within the system.

4. **Desertification and Soil Degradation Combat:** In areas where soil is degraded or unsuitable for agriculture, hydroponics and aquaponics offer an alternative solution for food production. Additionally, as they don't rely on soil, they don't contribute to erosion or

salinization, common problems in many parts of the world.

5. **Local Production and Reduced Transportation Emissions:** Hydroponics and aquaponics, being suitable for urban agriculture, allow food to be produced closer to consumption centers. This reduces the need to transport food over long distances, thus cutting emissions related to transportation.

6. **Bioaccumulation and Sustainable Fishing:** In aquaponics, the use of fish as a nutrient source can help alleviate pressure on fishing in natural ecosystems. When properly managed, these systems can sustainably produce fish, reducing the need to fish in marine or freshwater ecosystems, which are often stressed.

7. **Climate Change Adaptability:**
Hydroponic and aquaponic systems, being largely controlled and shielded from extreme weather conditions, offer a resilient solution to climate change. As external weather conditions become more unpredictable, these indoor systems can continue to consistently produce food.

In conclusion, while hydroponics and aquaponics also present challenges, such as the energy required for operation or the choice of appropriate materials, their potential for sustainability and positive environmental impact is substantial. They represent a promising avenue to address some of the most pressing agricultural and environmental challenges of our time.

Automation and Technology in Hydroponics and Aquaponics:

1. **Electronic Monitoring:** With advanced sensors, it's now possible to monitor various water parameters like pH, electrical conductivity (EC), and oxygen levels in real time. These sensors can send automatic notifications when values deviate from optimal ranges, enabling timely interventions.

2. **Apps and Software:** Specific apps and software for hydroponics and aquaponics help farmers track daily operations, plan harvests, and analyze production data. These applications can also integrate with sensors to provide a centralized monitoring platform.

3. **Smart Lighting Systems:** LED grow lights can now be programmed to emulate the solar cycle, providing plants with the optimal lighting

needed for different growth stages. These systems can also adjust light intensity and wavelength based on specific plant requirements.

4. **Automated Feeding Systems:** Automatic dosing pumps can deliver nutrients and solutions to the hydroponic or aquaponic system accurately, based on data collected from sensors. This ensures that plants receive the right amount of nutrients consistently.

5. **Robotics:** Developing robots designed to perform tasks like seeding, pruning, and even harvesting in hydroponic and aquaponic environments. These solutions can reduce the need for human intervention and increase efficiency.

6. **Artificial Intelligence (AI) and Machine Learning:** AI can analyze

data from sensors and other sources to optimize growth conditions, predict issues or diseases, and even forecast harvests. Machine learning can help systems "learn" and adapt over time to specific crop needs.

7. **Augmented Reality (AR) and Virtual Reality (VR):** These technologies can provide growers with 3D visualizations of their structures, assist in space planning or troubleshooting, and offer immersive training for new farmers.

8. **Future Innovations:** While vertical farming and smart greenhouses are already becoming mainstream, the future might see the integration of biotechnologies like genetic modification to create plants optimized for growth in hydroponic or aquaponic environments. Renewable

energy sources like solar or wind could power these systems, making them even more sustainable.

9. **Automated Cooling and Heating Systems:** Depending on the geographical region and climate conditions, maintaining a constant temperature inside a hydroponic or aquaponic system can be crucial. Automated heating and cooling systems can regulate water and air temperature to maintain ideal conditions, maximizing plant growth and fish health.

10. **Advanced Water Filtration:** Modern technologies offer increasingly efficient water filtration systems, crucial for removing impurities, regulating nutrients, and ensuring a healthy environment for both plants and fish. UV filtration, for

example, can help neutralize harmful bacteria and pathogens.

11. Droni and Cameras: Aerial surveillance using drones can provide a clear picture of large hydroponic and aquaponic structures, facilitating plant health monitoring and rapid identification of any issues. Underwater cameras, on the other hand, can be used in aquaponic systems to monitor the health and behavior of fish.

12. User Interface and Dashboards: Developers are creating intuitive dashboards that allow farmers to have an overview of their system in a single screen. These panels can display real-time data, trends, alerts, and forecasts, offering users a more streamlined and proactive management of their setup.

13. Internet of Things (IoT) Integration: IoT-connected devices can communicate with each other, enabling a constant flow of data and the automation of various functions within a hydroponic or aquaponic system. This interconnectivity can increase efficiency, reduce waste, and improve yield.

14. Backup and Security Systems:

With increasing dependence on technology, it's essential to have backup systems in case of failures or power interruptions. Generators, backup batteries, and alarm systems can ensure that hydroponic and aquaponic systems continue to function smoothly, protecting the investment and ensuring production.

15. Online Training and Resources:

With the advent of digitalization, there are more and more online platforms dedicated to hydroponic and aquaponic training and information. Webinars, courses, forums, and blogs offer enthusiasts and professionals a wealth of knowledge and a place to share experiences and challenges.

In conclusion, technology is playing a crucial role in the evolution of hydroponics and aquaponics, taking these agricultural methods to the next level of efficiency and sustainability. Integrating these technologies requires an initial investment, but the long-term benefits in terms of productivity, resource savings, and sustainability can far outweigh the costs.

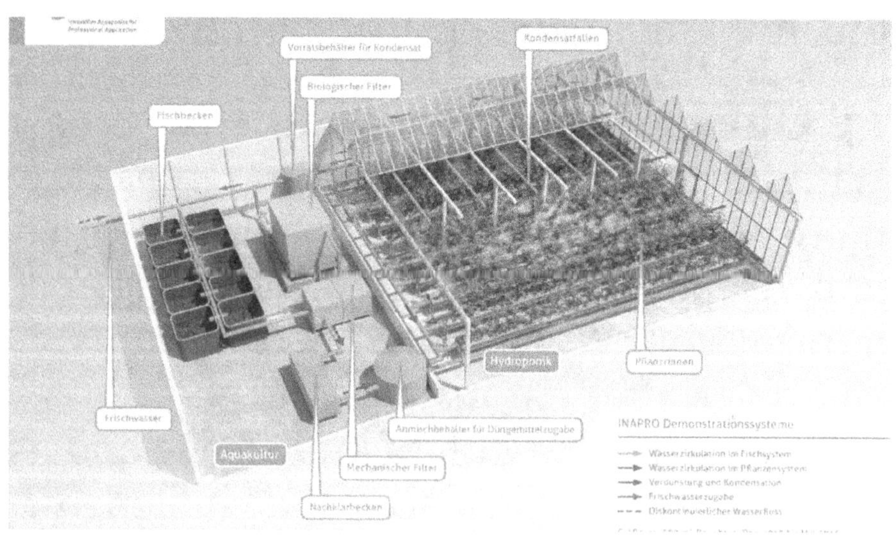

Costs, ROI, and Economic Considerations in Hydroponics and Aquaponics: In-Depth Details

1. **Initial Investments:** a. **System Setup:** Depending on the size and complexity of the chosen system, initial costs can vary significantly. This includes tanks, substrates, pumps, lighting, heaters, and other essential components. b. **Purchase of Fish and Plants:** For aquaponic systems, the initial purchase of fish can represent a significant cost. Additionally, the selection of seeds or seedlings for cultivation can vary based on prices. c. **Technology and Automation:** The incorporation of advanced monitoring and control systems can increase initial costs, but often these systems can enhance efficiency and reduce long-term operational costs.

2. **Operating Costs:** a. **Energy:** Energy costs for pumps, lights (if used), heating, and other devices can constitute a significant portion of operating expenses. b. **Nutrients and Fish Feed:** The ongoing supply of nutrients for hydroponic systems and fish feed for aquaponic systems represents recurring costs. c. **Maintenance:** Even though hydroponics and aquaponics may require less labor compared to traditional agriculture, there are still costs associated with regular maintenance, cleaning, and replacing worn parts.

3. **ROI Calculation (Return on Investment):** a. **Break-Even Point:** Determining how long it will take to recoup the initial investment through sales and production. This can help in financial planning and

setting goals. b. **Price Evaluation:** Considering the market and deciding if hydroponic or aquaponic products can be sold at a premium compared to traditional products. c. **Continuous Monitoring:** Using software or spreadsheets to constantly monitor operational costs and revenues, allowing adjustments based on market conditions and operational challenges.

4. **Additional Economic Considerations:** a. **Grants and Incentives:** In many regions, there may be government incentives or grants available for farmers adopting sustainable methods like hydroponics and aquaponics. b. **Indirect Cost Savings:** Efficient water use, reduced pesticide use, and lower land requirements can lead to significant long-term savings. c. **Diversification:** The ability to grow

different varieties of plants (and fish, in the case of aquaponics) can offer protection against market fluctuations and increase income stability.

5. **Economies of Scale:** a. **Unit Cost Reduction:** The larger the operation, the greater the capacity to reduce unit costs, as purchasing resources in larger quantities can lead to discounts. b. **Infrastructure:** A larger configuration might require more automation, and while this could mean a higher initial investment, it can lead to significant savings in terms of labor and efficiency over time.

6. **Training and Education:** a. **Courses and Seminars:** Participating in courses, workshops, and seminars might involve initial costs, but the knowledge and skills

acquired can lead to more informed decisions and better system management, reducing costly errors.
b. **Consultation:** Engaging specialized consultants in hydroponics or aquaponics can help optimize operations and avoid potential obstacles.

7. **Marketing and Distribution:** a. **Branding and Promotion:** Establishing a strong brand and promoting the benefits of hydroponically or aquaponically grown products can help command premium prices in the market. b. **Distribution Channels:** Investing in efficient distribution channels and logistics strategies may involve initial costs, but ensures that products reach customers in the freshest and quickest manner possible.

8. **Insurance and Risk Management:** a. **Insurance Coverage:** Protecting the investment from potential calamities, such as electrical failures, diseases, or natural disasters, is crucial. Although representing an operational cost, it provides essential security. b. **Contingency Planning:** Implementing emergency plans and anticipating risk scenarios can help mitigate losses in unforeseen circumstances.

9. **Long-Term Financial Considerations:** a. **Depreciation:** Factoring in the depreciation of equipment and infrastructure over time. While some equipment might have a lifespan of years, others might require more frequent replacements. b. **Renewal and Upgrades:** The hydroponics and aquaponics industry

is rapidly evolving. This means that new technologies and methods might become available, and investing in such innovations can help keep the operation at the forefront. c. **Forecasting and Budgeting:** Effective financial planning and creating an annual budget can help predict and manage expenses, ensuring the operation remains profitable. By incorporating these considerations into financial planning and the management of hydroponic or aquaponic operations, farmers and entrepreneurs can navigate the economic landscape more effectively, maximizing ROI, and ensuring the long-term sustainability of their businesses.

14. Innovative Approaches for Cost Reduction: a. **Renewable Energy:** Adopting renewable energy sources such as solar or wind power can involve a high initial investment, but it significantly reduces long-term energy bills and may even qualify the operation for subsidies or government incentives. b. **Cooperative Purchasing:** Forming or joining agricultural cooperatives can allow farmers to collectively purchase resources like nutrients, equipment, or even fish, thereby reducing unit costs.

15. Scalability and Expansion: a. **Modular Investments:** As expansion becomes a consideration, opting for modular systems can enable a gradual increase in production without a massive capital outlay. b. **Experimentation and Research:** Allocating a portion of the budget for experimenting with new methods or technologies can help identify best practices that can enhance profitability.

16. Portfolio Diversification: a. **High-Value Crops:** Exploring crops with high market value or that are rare in the region can lead to higher profit margins. b. **Secondary Products:** In addition to main crops, consider producing secondary products like ornamental plants, herbs, or even natural cosmetics based on plant extracts.

17. Obtaining Funding and Grants: a. **Government Programs:** Many governments offer subsidies or low-interest loans to promote sustainable agriculture and innovation. Being aware of and leveraging these opportunities can significantly reduce startup or expansion costs. b. **Crowdfunding and Private Investors:** Crowdfunding platforms or seeking investors interested in sustainable agriculture can provide the necessary capital to start or expand an operation.

18. Supplier Relationships and Supply Chain: a. **Negotiations and Long-Term Contracts:** Establishing strong relationships with suppliers can lead to discounts or favorable payment terms. Also consider entering into long-term contracts to ensure price stability. b. **Exploring Alternative Sources:** Continuously seeking alternative suppliers or production methods can lead to discovering more cost-effective or efficient options.

19. Cost-Benefit Analysis: a. **Periodic Analysis:** Regularly conducting cost-benefit analyses can help identify areas of waste or inefficiency in the system and guide investment decisions. b. **Comparison with Traditional Systems:** Maintaining an understanding of cost dynamics in traditional agriculture can provide insights into the value and benefits of hydroponic and aquaponic systems.

20. Labor Considerations: a. **Training and Education:** Ongoing training for workers may seem like a cost, but it enhances efficiency, reduces errors, and can even elevate the value of products in the market. b. **Automation:** Where possible and financially viable, investing in automation to reduce long-term labor costs.

Through a thorough understanding and analysis of economic and financial variables, entrepreneurs in the field of hydroponics and aquaponics can optimize their operations, ensuring not only ecological sustainability but also economic sustainability.

21. Location and Logistics: a. **Leasing vs. Purchase:** Choosing between leasing or purchasing land can have profound economic implications. While purchasing involves a long-term commitment and greater flexibility, leasing can reduce initial costs and offer more mobility. b. **Proximity to Markets:** Positioning near target markets can significantly reduce logistical costs, particularly for products that need to be delivered fresh.

22. Certifications and Quality Standards: a. Investing in Certifications: Obtaining certifications like "organic" or "sustainable" can increase the perceived value of products, allowing for premium pricing. b. **Quality Monitoring:** Implementing rigorous quality control systems can reduce losses due to defective or contaminated products, while also ensuring consumer trust.

23. Marketing and Branding: a. Tell the Story: Effective branding for a hydroponic or aquaponic company can involve sharing its unique story, sustainable approach, and the benefits of soilless cultivation. b. **Direct Sales Channels:** Consider direct sales methods such as farmers' markets or online sales. This can increase profitability by bypassing distributors.

24. Risk and Crisis Management: a. Insurance: Being adequately insured can protect an operation from losses due to natural disasters, diseases, or other unforeseen events. b. **Contingency Plans:** Having detailed plans for addressing various crises, from technological failures to epidemics, can mean the difference between a temporary setback and a business catastrophe.

25. Networks and Partnerships: a. **University Collaborations:** Collaborating with academic institutions can provide access to cutting-edge research, student internships, and training opportunities. b. **Industry Groups and Associations:** Joining or forming industry groups can provide support, resources, and a stronger voice when interfacing with government entities or negotiating with major suppliers.

26. Long-Term Considerations: a. **Succession Plans:** Especially for family-owned businesses, having a plan for who will take the reins ensures a smooth transition and business continuity. b.

Geographical Expansion: As an operation becomes more stable, consider opportunities for expanding into new geographic areas or markets.

Each point listed represents a series of strategic decisions that operators in the field of hydroponics and aquaponics must make. The key to success in this innovative sector lies in carefully balancing costs with benefits, leveraging new technologies and methods, and remaining focused on quality and sustainability.

14. Conclusion: The Future of Hydroponics and Aquaponics Sector Growth Prospects:

Hydroponics and aquaponics are experiencing a golden age, and this trend is set to continue. Several motivations fuel this growth: • Demographic Growth and Urbanization: The increasing global population and growing urbanization require innovative solutions to meet food demand. Urban agriculture, including hydroponics and aquaponics, addresses this challenge by allowing food to be grown close to consumption areas. • Food Security: The ability to cultivate in controlled environments reduces reliance on external weather conditions, ensuring more predictable yields and lowering the risks of diseases and pests. • Environmental Sustainability: Both systems, if managed correctly, can use significantly less water than traditional agriculture and reduce the need for chemical pesticides and fertilizers.

Future Opportunities and Challenges: • Technology and Research: Technological advancement will continue to influence the sector, bringing new solutions for monitoring, automation, and crop optimization. Research, both academic and industrial, will deepen our understanding of plant-fish relationships, leading to even more efficient systems. • Integration with Other Technologies: Vertical farming, often utilizing hydroponics, presents a particular opportunity. This form of agriculture can maximize food production in confined spaces, making it ideal for urban areas. • Training and Education: One obstacle to sector growth might be a lack of proper training. Offering courses, workshops, and other educational resources will be essential to ensure that farmers have the necessary skills. • Regulations and Standards: Like any rapidly growing sector, hydroponics and aquaponics might face challenges related to new regulations. Sectoral organizations and stakeholders will need to work together to ensure any new laws are balanced and sustainable.

In summary, the horizon for hydroponics and aquaponics is bright, but not without challenges. However, with innovation, collaboration, and a commitment to sustainability, these systems have the power to revolutionize how we think about agriculture and food production in the 21st century.

Socio-Cultural Aspects and Public Acceptance: The transition to alternative agricultural methods like hydroponics and aquaponics requires not only technological but also cultural revolution. • Consumer Education: While some communities enthusiastically embrace these methods, others may be skeptical about the safety and quality of foods produced in such systems. Highlighting research demonstrating the healthiness and nutritional quality of hydroponically and aquaponically grown foods can help alleviate these concerns. • Aesthetics and Perception: Traditionally, the perception of a farm is that of a place with vast fields under the sun. The idea of growing food in greenhouses or buildings might not align with this romantic image. However, through guided tours, educational days, and effective marketing, the public can come to understand and appreciate the value of these innovative methods.

Scalability and Personalization: A significant aspect of these techniques is their scalability. While some operations can cover extensive spaces and produce food on a large scale, other systems can be small, suitable for home or tight urban communities.

• Home Hydroponics and Aquaponics: The trend toward food self-sufficiency and urban farming is growing. Home hydroponics and aquaponics offer opportunities for individuals and families to cultivate their own food in limited spaces like balconies, terraces, or even indoors. • Customization for Specific Cultivation: Each plant has different needs in terms of light, nutrients, and pH. Technology and research will allow for greater customization, enabling farmers to adapt their systems to optimally grow specific plant varieties or fish breeds.

Innovations in Materials and Design: With the increasing popularity of hydroponics and aquaponics, there will be a push for innovation in system design and the use of sustainable materials.

• Biodegradable and Recyclable Materials: Plastic is prevalent in current hydroponic and aquaponic systems. However, with a focus on sustainability, we might see greater adoption of biodegradable or easily recyclable materials to reduce environmental impact. • Innovative Designs: Aesthetics and functionality can go hand in hand. As farmers seek energy-efficient solutions, designers can create systems that are not only functional but also visually appealing, seamlessly integrating into urban spaces.

In conclusion, while hydroponics and aquaponics have already made significant strides, the future holds many opportunities and challenges. The intersection of technology, biology, design, and culture will create an exciting era for agriculture in the future.

15. Appendix: Resources and Practical Guides

In this rapidly growing field, resources abound for those looking to delve deeper or start their own hydroponic or aquaponic project. Below is a curated selection of reliable resources.

Books:

1. "Hydroponics for Beginners" by Marco Rossi: A comprehensive guide explaining the basic concepts of hydroponics, ideal for those new to this technique.

2. "Aquaponics: The Art of Growing Fish and Plants Together" by Luca Bianchi: This book details how to create a sustainable aquaponic system, with practical advice on plants and fish.

Courses:

1. "Hydroponics and Aquaponics: The Green Revolution": An online course

covering both theory and practice, offering video lessons, course materials, and expert support.

2. On-Site Workshops: Many agricultural centers and universities offer workshops and intensive courses for those seeking hands-on training.

3.

Associations:

1. National Hydroponics and Aquaponics Association (ANIA): An organization that promotes research, provides training, and represents the interests of hydroponic and aquaponic farmers.

2. International Hydroponic Farming Federation: With members from around the world, this federation provides a platform for knowledge and resource sharing.

Online Resources:

1. HydroForum: An online forum where hydroponics enthusiasts can ask questions, share experiences, and receive advice from experts.

2. AquaPedia: An online platform dedicated to aquaponics, featuring guides, articles, and video tutorials.

3. Plant Database: An indispensable resource listing the specific requirements of various plants, helping farmers choose and cultivate successfully.

Step-by-Step Guides:

1. "Creating a Home Hydroponic System": A detailed guide covering everything from choosing the right container to installing lights and pumps.

2. "Introduction to Aquaponics for Beginners": This guide offers an

overview of the essential components of an aquaponic system and provides step-by-step instructions on how to start it.

In conclusion, whether you're looking to start a small hydroponic garden on your balcony or planning to establish a commercial aquaponic farm, resources are available to assist you at every step of your journey. This appendix serves as a starting point, but the key is continuous research and learning in this evolving field.

15. Appendix: Resources and Practical Guides (Extension)

Hydroponics and aquaponics are growing disciplines, with an increasingly active community and abundant resources. For those looking to dive into these worlds or for those wanting to deepen their knowledge, here's a more detailed overview of available resources.

Conferences and Events: • International Hydroponics Symposium:

An annual event bringing together global experts in the field of hydroponics, offering presentations, workshops, and networking opportunities. • Aquaponics Expo: This annual exhibition showcases the latest technologies and innovations in aquaponics, featuring live demonstrations and Q&A sessions.

E-Learning Platforms: • HydroLearn: An online learning platform specialized in hydroponics courses, offering modules from beginner to advanced. • AquaU: An e-learning website exclusively dedicated to aquaponics, with interactive courses and case studies.

Blogs and YouTube Channels: • HydroBlog: A blog covering the latest trends in hydroponics, with product reviews, tips, and tricks. • AquaFarm Channel: YouTube channel offering video tutorials on setting up and managing an aquaponic system, expert interviews, and tours of successful aquaponic farms.

Apps and Software: • HydroApp: A mobile application helping hydroponic farmers monitor their systems, with maintenance reminders and a library of common issues and solutions. • AquaTech Suite: Computer software offering advanced tools for designing, simulating, and managing aquaponic systems.

Communities and Groups: • HydroCommunity: An online community where hydroponics enthusiasts can share their experiences, ask questions, and receive advice. • AquaGroup: Facebook group dedicated to aquaponics, with members from around the world sharing photos, success stories, and solutions to common problems.

Suppliers and Specialized Shops: • HydroShop: An online store offering a wide range of hydroponics products and equipment, with customer reviews and technical support. • AquaGoods: A leading supplier of aquaponics equipment, with a wide range of products and detailed guides on how to use them.

In the world of hydroponics and aquaponics, resources continue to multiply at an incredible rate. This extended appendix provides a deeper overview of what's available, but as always, the key to success in these fields is ongoing education and experimentation.

Conclusion: Revolutionizing Agriculture with Hydroponics and Aquaponics

The journey through the universe of hydroponics and aquaponics has unveiled a captivating reality: the possibility of cultivating food in revolutionary, sustainable, and highly efficient ways. We've explored the basic principles, equipment, advanced techniques, and economic and environmental considerations. These cultivation methods represent not only a solution to the challenges of traditional food production but also a hope for a future where agriculture can be integrated into urban fabric, reducing our ecological footprint.

Summary of Key Points:

1. Introduction to Soilless Cultivation: The importance of finding alternatives to traditional cultivation due to growing food demand and environmental challenges.

2. Basic Principles of Hydroponics: The science and benefits of growing plants using nutrient solutions instead of soil.

3. Basic Principles of Aquaponics: Combining aquaculture and hydroponics, harnessing a symbiotic ecosystem between fish and plants.

4. Components and Equipment: The fundamental infrastructure needed to implement these techniques.

5. Popular Hydroponic Systems: Analysis of widely-used techniques and their pros and cons.

6. Setting Up an Aquaponic System: Considerations for choosing fish and plants and creating balance in the ecosystem.

7. Nutrition and pH: The criticality of monitoring and balancing nutrients and pH to ensure optimal plant growth.

8. Pest and Disease Management: Preventive and therapeutic strategies in a soilless environment.

9. Integration of Hydroponics and Aquaponics: How to combine the strengths of both methods to optimize production.

10. Case Studies and Commercial Successes: Concrete examples of success in the field.

11.   Environmental Impact and Sustainability: The enormous potential of these techniques to reduce resource usage and enhance sustainability.

12.   Automation and Technology: The advent of technological innovations in the sector.

13.   Economic Considerations: Understanding ROI and navigating through required investments.

14.   The Future of Hydroponics and Aquaponics: An overview of emerging trends and future challenges.

15.   Resources and Practical Guides: A guide to further immerse yourself in the topic and continue learning.

Useful Resources:

Websites:

• Hydroponic Society

• Aquaponics Association

Books:

• "The Complete Guide to Hydroponic Farming" by Paul Simmons

• "Aquaponic Gardening: A Step-by-Step Guide" by Sylvia Bernstein

Forums and Communities:

• Hydroponics Forum

• The Aquaponics Community

We encourage you to further explore these resources and to experiment on your own. The future of agriculture could be greener, more efficient, and more sustainable thanks to methodologies like hydroponics and aquaponics. The key is knowledge and a willingness to innovate. Happy cultivation!